The Minnow Catching Boys

The Minnow Catching Boys

by

Susan Skinner

HEADLAND

First published in 1995 by HEADLAND PUBLICATIONS North Wales and Wirral

Ty Coch, Galltegfa, Llanfwrog, Ruthin, Clwyd, LL15 2AR and
38 York Avenue, West Kirby, Wirral, Merseyside, L48 3JF

ISBN O 903074 93 1

ACKNOWLEDGEMENTS

Acknowledgements are due to the editors of the following books and magazines in which some of these poems first appeared: Envoi Tandem Weyfarers The Woman Journalist Poet's England Striking Statues A Groat's Worth of Wit Both Sides of the River The Unheeded The Woman Journalist

To Ken with love

Contents

(Cont.)

Contents (Cont.)

The minnow catching boys

The Minnow Catching Boys

By the bridge the sunburnt boys,
knee-deep, with yellow nets on sticks,
waylay the silky edge of water,
scan and dip.

Heads down, brown necks glistening
they make bets, poke and tip
their nimble catch.
Then one boy delicately lifts

his net and treads
the wet ridges of stone
to the dry pebbles, flips
his minnows into a tin bucket

and wades back slowly, alone
with a sense of immortality.
For they have always been here,
the minnow catching boys,

breeches rolled, hands cupped,
feet green in the shallows,
followed by an old dog bearing
a stick from ear to ear

and a small girl
who can never quite catch up,
calling for them to wait.
But no-one waits.

The dog paddles to the beach,
shakes in a cascade of diamonds
then wanders off.
Shadows under the bridge unfurl

and slip down river; the slow
sun dips behind trees
in a green burying.
And when they have had enough

the minnow catching boys
make for home, swinging
the tin bucket, shouldering nets
that glint like yellow butterflies in tow.

Breaking Bread

The harbour shines,
ovals of light skim the water's
shift and slop.
Where jade fish hide
boats swing and stop.

Swans give up their grace,
paddle ashore.
Ducks sparkle the hem
of stones, bob and gabble
like the child who feeds them.

Out of the huge sky
and windy weather
a stack of sunshine
drops on the greedy head
of a white white swan

as if to celebrate
the coming together
of child and bird,
a familiar and never solemn
breaking of bread.

Out of Bounds

We sleep above the horses
beautiful silent creatures
from another world.
The night is cool moon air,
the horses below
primitive companions
of our slow dreams.

Lightly at daybreak
bright hard sounds
clutter the window;
girls have come to rake
and steep the cobbled yard
in hosannas of water,
water down our sleep.

The horses are led out
into their own fields
tipped with buttercups and sunlight.
One trains on a long rope
others gallop free
and those that crop the grass
have shining backs.

Later we climb the downs;
a green-grey sea
overflows the horizon.
Fields pitch on the side of the hill
where the horses lean,
small and clear like cut-outs.
No clouds take the sun.

Time that grows everywhere
suddenly tucks in,
tiny as a daisy.
We are always on summer's ground
When we return
the horses are on the alert
as if they know we have been out of bounds.

The Holy Vestment

Imagination is a holy vestment,
who wears it on his skin keeps warm.
Even in the grove of skeletons
he walks unharmed.

The dead are always old
like the bare bony moon
in the sky's dark grave.
But when the holy vestment touches them
they dance, they shine, drawn
into its tender wools of grass
its blue day threads:

so this is the summer place
the zigzag path, the lawn,
where once we sprawled and beside us,
bicycles, shining, flung down
as if we were the owners.

Unaware we owned nothing,
not even our grassroot dreams
or the dust we sent up as we rode on
and on towards the grove of skeletons.

Secret Haven

Do not disclose your haven:
undeclared,
it will remain at hand,
a private rapture.

Others may capture it,
take it to a land
of snow and grief,
abandon it,

and when you travel
the journey of its loss,
forget why you have gone
and where.

Unless your haven is everywhere,
the stone in the well,
the star over the mountain,
do not tell.

South Bank at Easter

Evening settles over the South Bank;
buildings topple into shadow, shadows
fall into the Thames like water weeds.

Musicians come to practise and below
Queen Elizabeth Hall the homeless move
like hidden roots: a girl in high boots

dress flowing like wings
kicks over the dustbins.
A boy with brutal stare

breaks up a dusty pile
of half-sawn planks - his missile
like an ill-made cross

falls into the Thames,
following the tide's ancient direction:
No chaos can push the cross upstream.

Quietly river baptises evening.
From the auditorium Bach's Passion
flies like a swan between cloud and falling sun.

For those who sing, love's royalty crowns them,
low water raises her lips. Outside
the girl and boy silently watch

city lights drop like pewter seagulls
into the river's black gullies.
The floating cross drifts

between frogs and water-lilies.
In old rhythms homing on the sea
their homeless angers drown: slowly, slowly,

peace comes in with the tide.
Even for them water raises her lips,
night erects a tent for their homecoming.

Exploring the City

I follow you through the city.
Every road leads to a waterfront
or an arch that spans the water
like an open-winged bird.
Gondolas edge the Grand Canal,
their shadows move and multiply.
We cross at the Rialto.

Shoppers bustle and plunder;
fruit and fish mosaic the stalls,
in shining windows bread becomes
a work of art.
We drink coffee in St. Marks Square
at Florians, like Thomas Mann.
Everywhere masks are for sale:

The long nosed bird is your favourite.
His forehead is wrinkled, his skin white.
You could be Jupiter or a feathered chieftain,
I, Minerva, or a lady behind lace.
We could buy a little mask
to put on the shelf
and imagine the Venetian Carnival.

We walk into the Ghetto.
Seven plaques to the Venetian Jews
who died in the unholy holocaust
bear witness on a plain brick wall.
Tenements are seven stories high.
A child cycles in the dusty square.
A lady opens her window to feed pigeons.

I follow you to the sea's edge.
We watch the boats sail away.
If you say,
let us take a boat to another island
I will follow.
Or is it I who lead you across the city,
to buy a ticket for the last port?

Safe Arrivals

When we cut adrift from Katmandu
to fly the frail hot air balloon
over Mount Everest,
our sherpas sport their coloured prayer flags
for safe arrivals.

We reach the base at sixteen thousand feet.
Our breath is arrow sharp.
Our radio balloons talk to the wind
for three white weeks.
Then the sherpas speak
the right words to the right gods

and out of nothing, bearing its moment of truth,
the wind swings across Everest
cradling our paper chariot of fire
and we rise like Icarus.
Someone shouts from the ground:
'May the winds welcome you, may the soft air
look after you.'

Everest is a shark in dark water.
Its grey scales grow and grow.
Its jaw is open.
Our balloon slips up the side,
a leaf, a bird,
spinning.

Yet in a single singing moment
we make our high arrival
cross the peak
cross the Styx -
for here Everest is bright as Heaven,
its white pastures glowing in the sun
the rest of life will always fall away.

Then our fuel gives out and we begin
to tumble down into the dark valley.
There will be no more safe arrivals:
We have no prayer flags,
no right words for the right gods
and surely they will kill our brave balloon
for its audacity.

Message

It hangs between a sun and moon,
tail end of that silver dust
curling like a snail;
a star of grace, the only one perhaps:
Holy star in a heap of stones.

Slowly, slowly out of its dark pod
hills crept on the sky's back,
valleys rippled,
seas leapt into the wind.
Amazing earth wove its own renewal:
flowers rose and fell like breath,
green leaves grew nightingales,
forests shadowed
silent tigers.
Grass bore man, a naked beast. At first
his bare heart wore the earth with care,
a little mantle over raging fires.
Then man put on a big head, careless hands,
clothed himself in power,
left his mantle threadbare, threw it down,
crushed it with his engine, spat on it.

And we, the disembodied wanderers,
voices of the universe who have
no marvellous cloth to weave,
had we the gift of tears, would weep
to see his star abused.

So take our message, whisper in man's ear.
His world is distant in its tiny shell
of dust, but it will draw you near.
It is a holy star, the only one
singing to itself.

Mandala

(from the Tibetan Exhibition at the Royal Academy 1992)

Monks from Tibet
know how to bless
the black tide.
Day by day
they make a mandala
from coloured sand.

With steady hands
they hold a horn to scoop
and tap the grains
in shelves
and singing shapes
that fly the pattern.

Every grain is itself
and a sign of the whole.
The lifting of sand,
the making of the pattern
is itself, and a renewal
of earth and sky.

When it is done
the monks carry the mandala
on its wooden board
down to the river Thames
where they release it.
Every grain sings

its own name
to the black tide.
The singing is countless
and the monks fly
their own words of peace
over the river.

Afterwards,
they walk lightly,
back to the building
where paintings hang
like beautiful
stuffed birds.

Star Tracks

Above the winter, stars mark out
their tiny campsites in the dark.
Universes back they shine,
steadfast across emptiness.
They tell us to be unafraid,
to light a fire on this lonely
camping ground and face the shining track
of time who bears the starlight on his back.

For we must all hold up a star
beneath the sky's great company;
and Time must move us to explore
and fly our fate, unravelling
its light, however small, that shines
clearly in its distant track
like these winter stars Time has made old
and turned their raging fires to points of gold.

The Rock

Night climbs the slippery sky
somewhere near Bakewell.
Humped like grazing sheep, green-grey,
grey-brown, hills wait,
already in the distance lose their way.

Outcrops of rain scupper the rock,
pitch into my back where I lie
face down, lost in the ill-defined
hills. Flowers stop up cracks, wind bossed
birds flutter my mind.

Under the blackening sky
this rock bears a million silences.
Its weight of birthdays dignifies my slack
red raincoat, the beat of my heart,
strengthens me to find a way back.

'Look,' say the voices of silence,
'darkness has its own map.'
As night caps the waterlogged air, I stand
to see the lights from Bakewell bloom
like flowers in the rain.

Stones

Stones have their songs too:
not immodest, like birdsong in May
when rain trickles to a standstill,
pigeons swish like puffing bellows through the air,
blackbirds choir,
but slow, silently gathered in,
silently stored:
Rhythms of ancient ploughshare,
thin chords
of flint waking fire.

Holiday Trees

Sun paws the Gate:
The city trembles.
Then trees are my green nursemaids, whisper
emerald water in their leaves,
shadow and shelter me.
Their branches shine like sealskin,
cradle sleep.

Then trees are my green godmothers,
offer me lemons,
yellow plums, green grapes,
orange blossom,
scents wandering down
layers of leaves,
air that wakes like inspiration.

They are my green counsellors
who bear high interwoven
fans of peace.
And faith that never moves
but roots unseen
under the city
where the lion stalks.

Summer Hill

Flints pack your green rump,
thread your spine,
roots vein your old ways.
Wolstenbury,
half asleep with time,

humped, head down
to water and windfall,
your earth burrows hold
the short tailed dreams of history,
its winter skeletons.

Today you are summerful:
daisies crimp, buttercups hold up
their sunny chins,
clover candelabras whiten grass
feathered by sunlight;

Ladies' slipper stand on shelves of shadow,
and where the candid briar rose
perfects the air
and is gone on a breath
foliage is transparent.

Trees wait; through high green woods
the sky is a thousand blue leaves.
Birds do not appear;
yet birdsong, intricate as lace
covers the wood.

Far off fields are misty,
landscapes float
weightless into air.
In a nest of trees the village
sings to itself.

Bubbles of time rise up from the church,
distant, self contained.
But you hold the old time:
across the valley
where the roads once were

scales of dragons glint and roar
and when low gliders
lean across your back
they fly the outline
of lost dinosaurs.

Separation

We are apart a thousand miles tonight.
Lost sheep, stars
sleep on the hill,
clouds open eagle wings.
The moon hides,
yet under blackness
she has kept her route:
a world away
the sun gives her light.

I open the window
as if you are still in the yard
looking up,
and remember
all the inept mortals
in the night
who take their unseen footsteps
by some light
a thousand thousand darknesses away.

From a Dutch Hotel

I left a garden of daffodils,
a landscape of catkins
and loose ends.

The hotel is a haven,
clean and quiet,
everything in its place.
But outside the window
lightning cracks,
thunder shouts,
snow softly pounds the canal.

I think of Dutch painting,
its two extremes:
figures in Bosch
distorted like graffiti
and those still interiors
where daffodils stand in jars
and through open doors
there are no loose ends.

Last Night in Cumbria

To Beatrix Potter

From your bed
you see white gulls flatter
the chalk grey sky.
You have written your last letter to the shepherd:
He was born here, he knows
every sheep has its own face,
every hill its own path.
It took you half a life-time to put on
the old rough overcoat of earth, to go
eccentric and behatted
like the Cumbrian sun.

When you were a child
freedom was a rabbit behind bars,
a fox you disembowelled.
Upstairs you made little books,
- sign post to fame and fortune -
but you were never fooled,
your business was always close at hand.
Tonight when your world is tied to the sun's mast
and sinks behind the hills,
it is the shepherd you have in mind,
his winter lambs.

Landscape with Poems

Where shadows and dried debris from the sea
tilt against the rocks, you read alone.
In the sudden sun your glasses gleam,
your floppy tramp hat whitens and above
the noise of visitors who choose ice-cream
tumbles down the cliff incessantly.

Your book is small, beleaguered by a thousand
thousand beaten pebbles and beyond
the dark primeval tide that rubs its slack
skin against the breakwater and tries
to grip the stones but foams and slithers back.
The sky walks on the sea and stretches upward.

From the open page and its cocoon
of small black strokes, you watch the poems rise
like fragile summer butterflies that draw
the heart because they brave a tide that eats
the world and fly old stones that crush the shore
and trust their beauty to one afternoon.

Words

Across empty air
they move mysteriously;
Euridice Pandora Helen sing
long after they are here.

Empires trail after
where words command,
their birthright powerful
like instinct, laughter.

They bind and loose, invisible
and strong: confine Caliban,
conjure Ariel.

Say 'death', death battens the day,
say 'love' love makes
a spring tree climb
out of clay.

Shadow

Shadow

You are the shadow on my bed,
duvet warm as a mother hen
dreams whole and round,
but you are in my head.

You are on my ground,
carpet soft to my feet
and no echo.
You do not make a sound.

You are a shadow at my meal,
subtle smells and wine lifting
glasses to the sun too high
for you to steal.

The walls of my house flout
the killing winds
where you always wait and I cannot
keep your shadow out.

Images

Huddled in the corner of my room,
one arm across your eyes, you do not look:
Gunfire is too loud, bread too rare.
Only the war dead rise to make you weep.

In my corner, deaf and blind from peace
I switch you off the screen, force you to leap
into its bankrupt pit. Outside, aloof
Midnight flowers catch the light and stare.

My frosty window flutters stars so sharp
they seem to cast black crosses in the air
and hooked above, the moon that sees us both
throws your crooked shadow from the roof.

War Field

Poor Tom's a-cold
his flesh is light
his bone juts out.
He sticks a straw pin in his hair,
whistles on the breath
to stop his mouth:
Where have all the flowers gone?
Night cataracts the brute of war and death.

All that shone
his grassy fields,their fruit,
his creatures of the sun and air
are trodden down.
Under an old tree
Tom hides his soul.
He slides into a dream, his summer fields
wear flowers like a wedding dress

and all in white
his bride glides over sunwet grass,
daisies in her hand.
Gunfire shoots,
it cracks
and petals fall.
The bride puts one flower
in Tom's bullet hole.

The Dream

Farm boy, soldier boy
From the English countryside,
Once the centre of your joy,
The ghost of spring is by your side.

Here where tents and sandbags graze
And tanks escape their sandy pen,
You innocently hitch your days
To the violent dreams of men.

War is a black sorcerer,
Where he goes he casts a stain,
His shadow is a murderer,
His hollow palm a grave of pain.

Tonight you dream that nature sets
her healing on insanity.
The desert drifts with violets
and the pale anemone.

Prisoner of War Camp

Nothing is left
but a flat stretch of grass
and in the dawn
ghostly prisoners
waiting to escape.

They gather under a chestnut tree-
its thick leaves
and upright blossom
waxed in moonlight.

When the moon goes out
and the tree-top sings
they dress themselves in daisies and cowparsley

and glide thin as rags
into the grass.

Sliding down the shadow line of time.

Poppies on Guard

November, Armistice Day.
By Westminster Abbey
Rows of poppies remind us
war is the enemy of youth.

A newspaper man shouts:
'Freedom in Berlin -
The Wall is breached.' Soldiers
smile in black and white.

Tonight in No-man's-land
people weep and make
ecstatic pilgrimage
into the West, while London

turns on tiers of light
against a hard November
moon, and bells ring out
a few faint stars. Silent

in the dipping shadows,
poppies guard the province
of the dead: their scarlet
regiments recall

how many freedoms bled
for Freedom's sake in No-man's
land, fifty years,
a wall of griefs ago.

Strawberry Fields

She who was born
to a delicate butterfly earth
is born in a ring of plague.
Her birthday bell broods,
rhythms of death
swaddle her cot.

Her window's barred,
outside the death man drags
his solemn cart.
'Throw out your dead.'
The dead patchwork the road.

Batlike her people
cluster in the dark
clutching at rags.
Her house is marked,
her iron door is starred.

Yet even in her captured infancy
she grows a dream
of strawberry fields whose scent
draws beads of blue green air
on summer's thread,

dangles butterflies and bees,
drowns earth in memories.
At night she leaps the spotted ring,
the dark dykes of death,
touches something free.

Prisoners

Thick with history's blood the wall
bludgeons a grey sky. A square,
high and black with bars is where
sad segmented heads look out,
three prisoners in masks, or are
they masks of prisoners? They stare
they do not move they do not shout.

The road is blind with cars and low
slurred reflections on the river
wave like water weeds that never
slip their roots; above a rail
half corroded by the water
light balloons with faces flower
from a long taut string. They sail

past the small black square like masks.
The prisoners pull them close and on
their tight skins write: LOVE HOPE and FREEDOM
Below the rush hour people freeze
into themselves and one balloon
-it is the sun- moves on and on.
Soon night will come when no-one sees.

Dead Eyes

Who were you killing,
dead eyes
with stone and stick and gun?
Anyone who cried?
God who walked away?
Your own heart downtrodden?
Who were you killing?

Who were you kidding
dead eyes?
Gun and stone and stick
gave you the final sick
fun when mercy lied
and you kicked pity down.
Who were you kidding?

Who are you kissing
dead eyes
with stick and gun and stone
screwed to the prison floor,
the driver missing?
Remembered daisies
make an iron chain.
Who are you kissing?

Things To Do

An old Devil you might say,
shouting, screaming,
'Don't contradict me.'
He sat with his legs dangling,
swollen up to the thighs.
The white frill of his pants,
tender, somehow,
and those legs unmarked
like a fat child's.
He would have no truck with doctors,
but the white child's legs
would not hold up much longer.
Later on the phone
he said I must never
make him lose his temper.
He said he did not mind
falling asleep forever.
But there were still things to do.

My Father's Death

On a no-breath
spirit becomes
death's mystery.
Not even the stars
are so mysterious.

Last night a window blew open,
a vase fell on its side.
You saw death come.
Why else did you pray
for your children, your parents?
Why did you say:
'Soon it will be a memory."?

All night your relentless heart
bore your sad body.
In the morning I crept in
to close the window.
You woke and shaved and dressed
and returned to your high chair
where you sat dignified,
in good humour.
You said to the nurse:
'Yes, yes! I quite understand.
I must go to a hospital or a home.'
And then you died.

My sister once told me
to listen to silence,
it has another sort of reality, she said.
Now it has come
on a no-breath.
We kneel to pray
knowing this moment is timeless,
that arrival and departure
are one and the same.

We pray for the soul of the dead
and we pray for ourselves who only understand
with head and heart and hand.

Memories

Gravestones, leaning by flint walls
or inlaid in wild grass
are quiet as shut doors; the central lawn
is a green prayer mat for birds.

Under autumn trees a bench
is splintered, grey with age.
My father sits in the cold sun, caught
by memories fragile as the light.

Behind him downs hump against winter,
clouds copy the wind.
At his feet spiders fabricate
their delicate walkways between flowers.

He points to a bare patch of ground:
There he will lodge
his memories, they will endure,
become the fabric of earth and its echo.

Kingswood Under Leaf

Who will remember Kingswood under leaf
with me, now you are gone?
Nothing has changed:
A few leaves perch on the bare boards
of a tree like winter birds,
but most leaves weep to the ground
without sound,
titian, russet, gold, yellow, brown,
spiralling down
to the wood awash with spent leaves,
where rainy earth soaks and sieves them
into muddy paths.

Seasons dance a double helix of life -
winter irreversibly linked to Spring -
so leaves have a replaceable beauty.
Likewise are you here
in the general unfolding,
the force that laid you fostering a new life?
Maybe; but I have seen
no phoenix surprising your grey gone ashes
floating soft green wings
like a Spring sky.
Your beauty is irreplaceable,
your death irreversible.
No-one remembers Kingswood under leaf
with me, now you are gone.

Villanelle for the Memorial Book

Made for the Childrens' Hospital,
Great Ormond Street, London

Though fate will draw its dice across the page
there is no writing yet, no black on white
to name the children who will never age.

This book is empty, save at every stage
the day, the month, the year, and pencil light
- though fate will draw its dice across the page -

thin lines ruled up that make a gentle cage
to guard the names of those who will take flight,
to name the children who will never age.

Below small flowers counterpoint the rage,
the grief of death, the falling down of night.
Though fate will draw its dice across the page

these flowers will give courage to engage
in memories of childhood, green and white,
to name the children who will never age.

Painted flowers delicately gauge
our link to nature, all its depth and height,
though fate will draw its dice across the page
to name the children who will never age.

Hospital Visit

I will not easily forget
the day they tied you to the seat
inside the ambulance and I
sat down beside your smiling feet.

All the way to Maida Vale
we sailed across the city's fleet
and when they lifted you on high
and brought you in from the grey street

your beauty filled the waiting room,
your slippers twinkled in the heat.
O Cleopatra, how they gazed -
the ones whom death and danger cheat.

For while they crouched like galley slaves
in patient rows, seat after seat,
somehow your presence turned the tide
and gave them victory in defeat.

For Barbara

For two days I only saw
the space you left,
black in a mountain range,
vertiginous hard shadow
between crags.

A long fall down
I dreamed of the shadow and the rose
and knew the shadow
places the rose in this world.

Then the rose became your work
and I saw you in your overall with deep pockets,
remembered your modesty, your determination,
the way you knew from experience.

Above my piano
Your swan floats delicately
detailed and perfect
under a timeless sky.
Your tree is a tangled
green Christmas on my shelf.

There should be no grief at your death.
It is only the shadow
of the gifts you left behind.
They hold your vision
and remind the eye.

Closure

(Rowley Bristow Hospital 1987)

We taught on Beatrix Ward
to the nurses' bleep,
the doctor's round, the tring
of telephones. Tame birds
sang in the wide window.

Our children were the ones
caught out,tumbled, tripped,
thumbs up to gravity.
For some godmother Fate
wore a crooked smile

at birth. Yet Peter learned
to write and James to read.
Andrew, Michelle, Carole,
all rang circles round
their wicked godmother.

Once in the hot sun
we talked of old Pompei
and Time who caught a child
half way up the stair
and left him there forever.

Big Stick Time, who joined
our class without permission,
stood up, beat his drum,
drew down the dusty blinds
and called for demolition.

My Pupil

Dolls' legs curled,
arms bent - thin as starvation -
body the size of a shoe box
but head and hands like everybody else,
you went to Lourdes and came back just the same.
When I asked you how it was, you smiled.
'My mind feels different.'
'How do you mean?'
'Without a trouble in the world,' you said.
Carol, whom I carry on one arm,
you teach me something I can never teach.

Striking Statues

Rocky has power in his mouth -
there lorries are locked, factories shut
between teeth clenched like a picket line.
Rocky has a big mouth.

Back at Head Office they wait:
Girls screw memos into paper sculptures,
gaze uselessly out of windows-
still mobiles behind glass.

The Boss has power
and Ben the Boss's mate
has words of strength.
For three days and nights
Ben and Rocky wage
words that slowly change
colour like those large
gobstoppers, smooth, round
and stone-like on the tongue.
Their factory towns listen
silent as statues.

Leaders and men sit in a hotel basement-
bunker charred with a thousand cigarettes.
Rocky's men are poor: memories
of soft sundays, pie and chips, hot baths
undercut the stench of word battle.

At two-o-clock on the third night
Rocky sounds the All Clear.
Words of peace are written down -
a Memorial to the battle.

Then Rocky calls the tune:
instantly factories are cleaned,
lines waltz in sequence to the formal
dances of production.
Lorries load and follow on each other-
doing the hoky-coky down the great
winding roads of England.

Next day the Boss and his men drink
to hide the devastation they still fear,
it is so close, broken imagery,
rubble giants picketing their minds.

Closed Factory:
Kirby Industrial Estate

The building is disjointed
work din gone
grass dislodges stone
barbed wire keeps the silence.

Once I heard them talk
undaunted, homely
in white overalls.
Their stories and words leapt
chutes of gravy, mountains
of peas, wavy puddings,
boxes that flapped open and shut
like kept birds.

KEEP OUT says the board. Yet some days
a white pigeon flies in from the city
to walk the gutter's shelf,
head tipped, listening.
No-one calls.

At nightfall a small ghost
flits across the roof.
Below lamp lights glisten: only
graffiti haunts the pitted wall.

The Wedding Photograph

A chance thing,
finding the sepia photograph
in the drawer,
brown and shining like an autumn leaf
pressed in an old book.
A chance thing, the wedding.
Here is my mother, smiling, her gentle face
under a slightly tipped brown hat,
a fur sloping down her shoulders,
a silk dress shafting to her ankles.
And father, handsome in his new suit
but unsettled, uncertain, more like a tomcat
put inside a cage.
And that is how it was,
witnessed by my grandfather,
his shoes shining, a time-piece on his belly,
and grandmother in tow,
surrounded by aunts, uncles and old friends
wearing wedding smiles
to cheer the lucky pair.

Mother and Father,
this brown photograph
puts your time into focus.
Yet you are always escaping
into our time,
smudging the heart,
standing at open doors,
beckoning.

The Shell

(1) The Journey

The sun lifts its hot mouth,
whispers in my right ear,
breathes on the mountain green fire.

At this party we keep our sorrows private.
The coach cradles us, its windows fly
streamers of wild flowers.

We sit like children
in the lap of the coach,
give up our freedom for a magic temple.

We cannot turn back:
Only the driver knows the way;
and the primitive sun.

but the guide has a secret route,
claps his hands, commands the coach to stop,
opens up the shell of time.

(2) At the Temple of Demeter

You run before us
apple bearing Demeter:
wild flowers are at your feet
and the wind rages.
Between pillars
clouds blow,
fleet as history
that has fleeced the temple,
broken sanctuary.
On falling ledges
birds nest
mountains sit.

Up on the hill the wind fights
the frail bones of visitors,
their fragile eyes.
You turn, goddess of Sicily,
smiling where orange yellow flowers
mingle with blue and mauve,
beckoning all those
who have watched their daughters
go down with the sun,
reminding them
that history's flight
is a mirage in Olympus.

(3) Alchemy

We rise early
and wait beneath the Judas tree.
The blossom is heavy,

its shadow fixed
into the dry inner sticks
of the tree, a dark

weight on the leaves.
But when sunlight
settles the horizon, seeps

into the hotel garden,
and the sun flies into blossom
like a bee, yellow with pollen

the shadow relents,
all our shadows are burnt
to gold in the Judas tree.

Crete

Green-glass waves shadow the seabed,
web its yellow sand.
Foam like rows of white spiders
jumps and shrivels on long beaches.
Naked people share the sun,
or sit under striped umbrellas.

Demi-gods haunt the taverna:
Ajax turns the meat,
Apollo revs his bike, Hephaestus
sits on a chair, wearing a black cap.
The beads dance when he laughs,
his eyes glint like a sword.

The Colonels' road runs between flowers.
Between sea and mountain
orange sellers wait, a peasant
jogs her donkey and a beekeeper
stumbles through the hedge wearing
a helmet like an astronaut.

The higher slopes bear a silver green
patchwork of olive trees,
a stocking stitch of firs - vegetation
fragile as embroidery.
Living under harsh mountains
the Cretans are not deceived

nor do they run away but pay respect
to the gods: for Zeus was bred
in a local cave and sometimes at first light
when the sun rises out of mist
their White Mountains are set apart,
shining, like Olympus.

Glass Beads

Glass beads of long ago
whose marbled colours rhyme,
sepia, blue, yellow,
beautiful with time,

Lozenge shaped and round,
light as the past is,
linking two thousand
three hundred centuries.

Long long ago,
a princess from the East
wore them, sepia, yellow,
Blue on her wrist

and held them in death's arm,
in earth's dark recess
to keep her spirit warm.
O trusting Princess.

Beneath my morning sun
their strange ancient bloom
glints as they summon
the princess from her tomb,

gleams when I hold them
in the hollow of my hand
with colours that stem
from the earth of her land.

Song

I took you to my little house
made you sleep without regret.
From your dreams I hid the cause
neither of us can forget.

Trees sing when the blackbirds pass,
Roses do not hold aloof,
fragrance folds into the grass,
rises to the grey slate roof.

Friend of shifting place and time
on these quiet days we stand
linked as rhyme is caught in rhyme,
smile to smile, hand to hand,

corded by the natural yoke
of sorrows we must bear with trust -
for your child who never woke
is no ordinary dust.

Born of a prolific nothing,
we have power to interpose:
Make a song from a bird passing,
a rose tree from a drifting rose.

Mrs. Lawrence's Vision

Alone, aloof, wary of unknown faces
Mrs. Lawrence lifts the lid of her bin:
bean and potato peelings slither in.
She thinks of Gert, untidy in her grave
who told her 'When the daylight fails, look up!'

Time falls behind.

In the narrow desolate sky
wild geese sound the last post.
Mrs. Lawrence turns to watch them fly
a v-shaped arrow, leaving lines of light,
like a tin opener, peeling off
the rind of dirty cloud, the smoke,
the unwashed moon, pale as a potato.
In the sky she sees a choir of children
fly round Gert who stands without her sticks,
in white, with shining wings!

The evening light takes fire.
Dusty leaves are little birds of gold,
a hundred window panes dissolve in flame,
chimney pots sprout trees and as the sight
of Gert in Heaven fades, Mrs. Lawrence
sees her T.V. aerial lean, tiptoe,
as if to fly after the wild geese
who draw their haunting arrow through the sky.

Poem for Helen's Baby

Take the baby's ear:
Milky skin, smell of newness,
open to a deeper source
than any words.
She who has listened to her own creation
hears the strange scratching of pens.
Is the babble of mutinous ideas
a threat to the simple thread
that binds her to the birds,
her earth-beat, the sound of her breath?
And when she is told later, that words explain,
will she be always slightly puzzled,
her ear waiting for the truth
she once heard?

Snapshots

On the day of my move the sun smiled like a mother,
took me for a walk in her blue garden
where bridal clematis softened the brick of my house.
I photographed Albert with his wheelbarrow -
larder of bread and vegetables he covered
with an old sack - 'I'm not a star every day,'
he said, but that day, his wheelbarrow was empty.

I photographed Lucy, still as a garden chair,
slippers odd, the shawl on her lap a crochet
of teen-age colours, face a map of age.
The sun showed me the way back to her childhood.
I photographed George leaning on the fence,
his patch of flowers a tangle of yellow scent
in the born again Spring.'I were born too soon,' he said.

I photographed mothers and children going up
to the downs to blow ghostly dandelions
into other fields. But I could not photograph
you as you waited by the big white van
and my life tumbled out of the house, locked
and put away for another time: you,
the silent ghost of my move, watching, watching.

Shakespeare's House:
New Place, Stratford-on-Avon

Last night by the flowing Avon
Prospero broke his magic stick,
drowning all his spells full fathom
five in fairy books whose quick

and potent words were first spoken,
here perhaps, where Shakespeare's rage
like Prospero's, turned to resignation
at the coming of old age.

Underneath the watered garden
New Place drowns: this broken wall
is all that's left, crabbed and sunk in
earth beside a covered well.

Yet I can see the poet walking
his green garden on a still
evening like this one, going
in and laying down his quill;

looking round him as he does
in Holy Trinity, with pride,
and after night fall, without fuss,
wandering by the river side

to let his haunting spirits loose.
They haunt us still, their love and grief:
Night after night, old Prospero's
drowned broken stick breaks into leaf.

Advertisement Love

On our side of the screen
there is only me
watching you
watching
Advertisement Love, an exotic creature
rising with the phoenix of music
from ashes of news
or some grey feature.

On a caribbean beach
coolcat reaches for her man
holds a mirror to her lips
walkabout on red red lipstick.
Teenagers with sunshine hair
swing and dance among the fans.
Go-getters and jet setters
wink and drink and kiss 'em quick!
Business girls subtitle scent,
spell seduction in slow motion,
on the catwalk youth free wheels
oozing love like suntan lotion.

On our side of the screen
there is only me
watching you
watching the television
and somewhere between
invisible, unclothed,
a love that could not bear
to see your chair empty.

Cat

How he purrs in my lap,
the cat you gave me:
yellow eyes squeezed in sleep,
mouth smiling.
You found him, or so you said,
in the London Underground,
half dead, fur fagged out,
thin as the mean lamplight
of the city line.
'Flea bag!' said the sharp green gossip
of underground lips.
But full of pity you lifted him up
and brought me my mangy burden.
I fed him on a daily diet
of poems and quiet
and now his breath rises and widens
and rings me round.
He has become a wise cat
my familiar,
my Buddha.
He teaches me stillness
and the sound of silence.

Water Rat

Cool, heavy water-rat,
in a fur swimsuit,
you remind me of the humans
who watch you from the bank.
They too wear inappropriate clothes,
move clumsily
through sun and shade,
dine off bright green tablecloths,
make for dark, sheltering holes
and disappear, like you, into a stream
that only goes one way.

The Lion Speaks

From the Lady with the Unicorn

Alone I guard this island, see you wait
far away. My upright banner bears
three bone sharp moons. I hold my tail alert,
my posture rampant near the queen who wears
a woven dress and sits between two trees.
She holds a mirror for her unicorn
and like a god he smiles at what he sees.
He lightly paws her lap, his slender horn
pointing to the pink and floral air
where rabbits run in play and small hares leap
for fun and hunting dogs smell flowers and deer
and fox go quietly. Alone I keep
a watch, but all who brave me and dare pass
will learn the secret of the looking glass.

Year's End

Corn is cut and bundled, roll on roll,
down the hillside winds and shadows bowl.
Hedgerow flowers, blue and red and white
dry to dun brown seed heads. Birds take flight.

We go indoors when dark day winter bears
the skeleton of Time and draw our chairs
closer to the fire as if to rhyme
its comfort with the transience of time.

Turn to half remembered memories
of flowers feathering the fields and trees
collaring the sun, when childhood cast
a simple light, and friends who wear the past

like secret shining badges and were born
with inky fingers and school uniform.
We sort out photographs and clothes and play
those tugging wistful tunes of yesterday.

The year has turned and shadows sharp as slate
lie on the yard where thin leaves jump and skate.
The drums of winter beat, its skeleton
is swinging from the window, looking on.

Domestic Love at Christmas

Above wide Christmas fields, darker, wider
night moved in like an armed rider,
black cloak flying back,
grey whip making stars crack
and spark - I thought of the night sky
as an unavoidable enemy.

What could I pit against its war games?
Only a vision that has many names,
none of the stranger
than the Child born in a manger.
Love, he said, is a flame that will reverse
the dark movement of the universe

its cold scenario.
I turned from the window
to watch you sleeping,
watch you a long time sleeping,
to stroke your head
and think of the other Child in the straw bed

until the window became
a glass division, a frame
round the wide, dark evening.
Or was it your love and trust
that turned the universe into a picture, a thing
I could take down and dust?

Snow Struck

Waiting for snow at Christmas
he looked out
for the land to turn white
birds to disappear.

He woke at midnight
to the slow filter
of stars and flakes.
By dawn the sky was clear,

his sleeping garden humped
in white fur,
his pond frozen,
reflections turned to marble, fish leaden.

The distant hill lay slack,
its road dumped,
too laden to leap in sight,
its high farm hidden.

Drifts had untacked the fields:
sheep stood still
grey on white.
The wood was deaf under its sack of snow.

He had no map for a white land,
nowhere to go
so when he saw
one left-over star,

a trick of light above the shining stack
of the buried farm,
he felt time lift its heavy arm,
beckon him back.

Cold Spell

Sky and hills have become
one under the snow,
roads are hidden.
Hedges grow shapeless
and other barriers merge
for those who have a landscape in common.
Doors open, fires blossom.

Outside children summon
their benign army
in nursery uniform.
A thousand snowmen wait
in parks and gardens.
Out of sight the sledge people shout
forgetting the burden of gravity.

It is a domestic time;
Between door and gate
the going is difficult
and the gate is hard to open.
Beyond we see nothing.
This cold spell, this unwritten white
takes us back to our beginning.